200
Stewardship
Meditations

Marshall Hayden

STANDARD PUBLISHING

Cincinnati, Ohio   3034

**Library of Congress Cataloging in
Publication Data**

Hayden, Marshall
  200 stewardship meditations.

  1. Stewardship, Christian — Meditation. I. Title.
II. Title: Two hundred stewardship meditations.
BV772.H36   1984   248.6   84-3
ISBN 0-87239-780-7

Contents

Introduction

Every week I have a thoroughly prepared, brief meditation before the offering is received, and I almost never preach a stewardship sermon. Occasionally I ask another in the congregation to lead the stewardship thought, but usually I ask for the privilege of leading it myself. With a two-minute meditation each week, I provide enough material for five sermons over a year's time!

One of the purposes of doing so is to teach giving and whole-life stewardship truths. We want the people to know about the Biblical concept of the tithe, about regular responsibility, and about the implications of being a living sacrifice. We also want to address people's emotions and touch their hearts.

Usually we do not jump into a celebration of the Lord's Supper without prayer or a quiet time and a carefully prepared Communion thought, to direct us to participation in a worthy manner and to point both our minds and our emotions to that high celebration. These suggested thoughts for offering time are designed to accomplish much the same thing—to focus our minds and draw our feelings to an important part of the church, and its life, and our Christian life.

Just a few suggestions as you approach the giving moment:

1. Be brief. Thirty seconds to two minutes will almost always be long enough to lodge one worthy thought.

2. Be positive. Even the music played at this time can be glad and moving. Giving can be a wonderful experience. It was for God.

3. Do not try to motivate people through fear, guilt, or high pressure. Such approaches might work well over a short term, but over a long term they can be unhealthy for a congregation.

4. Watch local newspapers for stories in everyday life that illustrate how we use our "things," in both good and bad ways.

5. Use warm humor; not belly laughs but thoughts that bring a chuckle and a twinkle.

6. Try to alert people to new arenas for their thinking about giving.

7. It is helpful to point out good examples—people who have used their lives and resources well, who have grown and were glad about it —but it is best to leave these people unnamed, and not to use yourself as an example of heroic giving.

8. Realize that you are working for a long-term development of stewardship sensitivity and a love of giving. Most of us come prepared with that day's offering, so you have little influence over the

offering for the day on which you speak. But you can help people as they prepare for the weeks, months, and years ahead.

Included in this little book are a collection of the meditations used with three congregations over the past twelve years. Some will be rather personal and may need to be adapted to your own congregation. Others are specifically intended for certain holidays or times of year.

It is my hope that you will find these thoughts helpful and that they might contribute to the health and happiness of your congregation. Feel free to use them in the way you believe to be the most profitable for the Kingdom enterprise we share.

— *Marshall Hayden*

The Source
and the Aim
of Our Giving

God's Giving

Recently one of the church's leaders made a commitment to a large goal being undertaken by his congregation. This leader is reluctant to tell what happened after that, lest we all think that God will always act just this same way. But the experience spelled out the truth again for him that "God will be no man's debtor." The day after he made the generous commitment, the surprise resolution of a business venture brought him the total amount of that commitment, plus $200.

If it is right, we shall do it; and God will give us the resources for working out the details.

Date Used: _____

"We have different gifts, according to the grace given us . . . if it is contributing to the needs of others, let him give generously" (Romans 12:6, 8).

Giving is one of the gifts of grace. The one who gives generously (or "with simplicity"—another translation) is practicing a gift that will develop other gifts and will be a reason for stunning spiritual growth. God makes provision for blessing those who exercise the gifts they are given.

Date Used: _____

Can I afford to tithe?

The church is right: That mission has a real need. That school fills a really important role. That service is important to a lot of people.

But can I afford to help?

Just about all of us have asked that of ourselves.

I wonder if God—as He put this place together, as He infused the good earth with nourishment, as He prepared to make the supreme personal investment, sending His Son—asked, "Can I afford this?"

Date Used: _____

We worry about inflation, everyday expenses, the cost of high-ticket items. Some of us may be functioning at a lower standard than at some time in the past.

But for how many of us is that true? How much do we really have? How long does it take to meet our obligations, as compared to several years ago? A quick trip to some sections of the city and country casts light on just how much we do have. News stories from other nations depict our affluence graphically.

We have much! It is a gift, and a stewardship, from God. Are we participating energetically and sacrificially enough in His business here and around the world?

Date Used: _____

A recent issue of a news magazine had an article about our "poor" millionaires—250,000 of them in the United States. A drive around the city or town will show you the remarkable second homes and recreational equipment many people have.

Not many of us are in these income categories, but we have a great deal. It comes from God. In part, today's gifts answer God's question, "Now what will they do with what I gave them?"

Date Used: _____

Sometimes we visit in a home and the folks there say, "At that last church all they talked about was give, give, give." It's great to be part of a church family in which we don't have to do that. You have just largely compelled yourselves. But in the business of God, that description isn't too far off. All God has done is "give, give, give."

Date Used: _____

Looking down from 30,000 feet, the clouds look like chunks of cotton. That view can help one think about God's world—the awesomeness of His power, the depth of His wisdom, and the width of His love.

How can we say thanks? Not very well! Our dedicated gifts today are one small expression.

Date Used: _____

11

God is the one who guides the accomplishment of His great purpose in the world. He answers prayers, meets people's needs, and makes the work of world evangelism happen. We, through our hands and our gifts, are often given the pleasure of being His agents. That is our privilege now.

Date Used: _____

"The only thing that goes faster than a teenage driver is a five-dollar bill."

We all shake our heads knowlingly. It seems we stay just one step behind the bills—and who doesn't want money from us these days?

Yet we live well. And who is the source of all we have? Our gifts today express recognition, and gratitude, and partnership in the eternal enterprise.

Date Used: _____

I suppose that most of us some time ago sensed the connection between the Lord's Supper and the offering. Maybe that's one reason that in the church they are traditionally close together.

Sometimes we sing the song "He gave His life, what more could He give?" Christ gave! His people rejoice as they develop that grace too.

Date Used: _____

Once upon a time there was a man who had nothing, and God gave him ten apples.

God gave him the first three apples to eat. The man ate the first three apples.

God gave him the second three apples to trade for a shelter from the sun and rain. He traded the second three for a shelter from the sun and rain.

God gave him the third three apples to trade for clothing to wear.

God gave him the last apple so that he might have something to give back to God to show his gratitude for the other nine. But the man looked at the tenth apple, and it seemed bigger and juicier than the rest. And he reasoned that God had all the other apples in the world. So the man ate the tenth apple and gave back to God the core.

God has given you enough apples to supply your needs—plus one with which you may show your gratitude to Him. The choice is yours. Will you return to God the largest and juiciest of your apples—or only the core?

Date Used: _____

Most of us have sung the chorus,

He owns the cattle on a thousand hills,
   the wealth in every mine.
He owns the rivers and the rocks and rills,
   the sun and stars that shine.

Then why doesn't He work out the operation of the church, the business of world missions, and the satisfaction of human need, without offerings? Because He has given me the privilege of being an essential partner in this important enterprise, and because I need to learn the joy of giving.

Date Used: _____

We Give First To God

"My father and mother ran a store in the East for years. One morning my dad answered the telephone and exclaimed, 'What? Picketing my store! What's come over them? They're my friends!'

"We rushed out of the house to the car. As we drove to town he asked, 'Does anyone pay higher wages? Or give larger bonuses? Why, I pay them when they're sick and help with hospital bills. What's come over 'em?'

"Just then we came in sight of the store. There was a large crowd in front and eight men marching around carrying signs. It was Mother who first realized the meaning of the scene. She read the signs aloud. MORE BOSSES LIKE OURS; WE WORK HERE AND LOVE IT; YOU CAN'T BUY FROM A NICER GUY. Her face was glowing, Mother turned to Dad. 'They're wishing you a happy birthday, dear.'

"Our attendance, our gifts, and our witness all say something like this—No Greater King than Ours; We Worship Here and Love It; You Can't Live With a Greater Hope."

—Thomas LaMance

Date Used: _____

A widely diverse collection of offerings will be given today: Some checks that will be headed off at the bank Monday morning; some gifts that are easily given from a comfortable supply; some bills sweaty from hands that have accepted them for hard work, smoothed them, and brought them today; some gifts still given a bit reluctantly.

All these are pieces of ourselves, which we give to God.

Date Used: _____

The sacrifices and offerings of the Hebrew people fed the Levites, built a big tent, and decorated the ark of the covenant. But they saw it as much more than that, and gave with remarkable generosity and joy. They gave to the glory of God.

Our gifts also build buildings, buy materials, and pay local and worldwide workers. It may seem rather common, but the commonness is changed

15

by the One toward whom all the giving is pointed. We also give with joy to the glory of God.

Date Used: _____

If we could give our offerings directly into the hands of God, that would be our choice. But He has always ordained that individuals and bodies of people (temple, synagogue, and church) carry out His bidding in the world and make use of what is given to Him. We listen, and we gladly bring a part of ourselves to the One who has given us all.

Date Used: _____

Today as you make your offering, shoot an instant's prayer toward one of the people touched by that gift—a missionary partner, a staff member, the congregation as a whole, students or people in their homes who are taught and stimulated by our materials, colleges, camp, homes for children and the aging.

Our gifts have personal significance; given to God, and touching other people.

Date Used: _____

God is watching. When plans are being made, be aware that God knows. When thoughts are being entertained, know that God knows. Confront God with your complaints and see what impression you come away with. Know that God watches and cares about your personal stewardship, too.

Date Used: _____

It's a marvel how God grows things in a garden. And that's the way the whole world is. With just a little work on our part, we are blessed with remarkable miracles. In this world that God has outfitted for our use, He wants the truth of an even grander eternity to be known. We have the job of telling that truth.

We Americans especially are gifted with unbelievable wealth. We give, today, not with the generosity God has shown, but with gladness and increasing maturity, to a fellowship committed to telling that truth.

Date Used: _____

Our gifts facilitate what the church can do, what it should do, and what it is committed to doing.

Yet, we remember that first we are presenting our gifts to God. That gives Him the highest glory. It gives us joy. It arrests us with the challenging reality of our responsibility.

Date Used: _____

We are trying to do better some things that we deeply believe are right for the people of Christ—to enlarge our witness, assist our study, and boost our opportunities for fellowship.

We are talking about doing our best for Christ, and we're determined to stretch past what we can see our way to do, knowing that if it is right the Lord will do what we cannot do (and we will have the privilege of being used by Him).

Date Used: _____

I can identify with a little boy in the Bible; the one who brought lunch to eat while he heard the Master talk about wonderful things. "Will you let the Master have your fish and bread to use?" the disciples asked him. And the little he had to give was used to feed thousands.

We may not have much to give, but we will not hold back what we have. And the Lord, who deserves all the credit, will make great things happen.

Date Used: _____

The Church's Need, Task, and Genius

The church believes in Christian education, family support, world evangelism, fellowship activities of Christians, physical buildings to house worship and study and fellowship, teachers teaching and preachers preaching, programs for spiritual body building, services for inspiration, keeping the church's communication among her people happening, and ministering to crises. Our gifts participate in all that, and more.

Date Used: _____

Sometimes we hear Christians say, "The church should do that!" or "The church will take care of that!" But who is the church?

We are.

When it moves forward, we are a part of that movement. When it stalls, we are a part to that. When it achieves victories, we are victorious. The church is not "they."

The same fact applies to the church's financial strength—resources for doing. We, you and I, are the church.

Date Used: _____

What would this world be like without the church?

I suppose that all of us have prayed, "Lord, thank You for commissioning the church. Its truth is our hope! Its ideals are the bulkhead of a sane society! Its fellowship is our joy! Its outreach is a flicker of life in a troubled world! It is a touchstone that calls us regularly to right! Thank You!"

Our gifts demonstrate the sincerity of our thanks.

Date Used: _____

We are God's servants to this area. We bring our committed offerings so that we might be part of a serving church—not to pay for the show, or to avoid the embarrassment of letting the plate pass by. My offering is my expression, in part, of being vitally involved in the church.

Date Used: _____

At every turn we find people with their hands out for our money. "Give to this!" "Buy this, you'll love it! You can't do without it." So we are a bit selective about how we handle it. We know that where our money goes, there our affections are.

The human end of the Lord's kingdom needs money to function effectively among people. Our gifts today express our affection.

Date Used: _____

We share a lot of good things in the church—
laughter, tears, urgent prayer, praise. We face tests
and crises together. We select from among ourselves
those who lead us. We have sent from ourselves
missionary partners around the world. It is
ultimately our responsibility, challenge, and
pleasure to keep this church growing and to
stretch its outreach and impact—not that of a
council, synod, executive group, or headquarters.
If we are to be the church we can be, under God's
direction we will do it. Our money commitments
are important to our life and strength as a church.

Date Used: _____

How can an imperfect institution like the
church—with its glory days, and its normal, plodding
times, and its fractured moments—represent the
eternal God? So human, yet divine? Should we
commit ourselves and our resources to this?
Yes! It's in God's plan. We can participate in
something much bigger than ourselves!

Date Used: _____

Follow your gift with attention, care, and prayer—
for the church as a whole, for the teachers into
whose hands materials are placed, for the members
of the church staff, for our missionary co-workers
and those working in Christian schools and

benevolent agencies, for kids on the bus and in camp and in youth groups, for those who plan and keep up the church properties—that it might be used with the best kind of stewardship.

Date Used: _____

A growing congregation needs so many things. Just like a teenager who keeps growing out of his clothes and needing bigger shoes, we need more equipment for study, more opportunites for healthy experiences, and more things to share with people around us.

Any parent knows that a growing child costs money. And a teenager (unless he is very unusual) does not have a lot of that stored up.

We give today because God deserves our return, and because we need the healthy experience of growing and giving. We also give because our grade-school-age church suffers those wonderful growing pains. As much as we can, we gladly share in that.

Date Used: _____

Some hard-nosed business people among us might have the nerve to ask, "Does it really pay to go to church?"

I could fold my hands and express pious horror at such an unspiritual and insensitive question, or respond in a stained-glass voice; "Why, certainly, in countless ways." And that is true, of course.

But let's note something a business person will understand. According to insurance companies, the person who goes to church regularly will live an average of 5.7 years longer.

At offering time, from the same business viewpoint, given a life expectancy of 72 years, you and I owe the church 7.9% purely from a fiscal perspective.

Zig Ziglar adds a couple of statistics and thoughts. "We also have approximately a 60% less chance of heart attack and 55% less chance of a one-car accident if we attend church regularly.

"A special note here to my non-Christian brothers, 'If you're not absolutely certain about where you are going when you die, I'd especially urge you to go to church regularly so you could at least delay your departure, because if you don't know Jesus, you've got it better here than you'll have it there.' "

Date Used: _____

A couple of years ago a series of humorous commercials was aired on television for Buick dealers. The same grizzled, finger-pointing fellow acted like he was the local dealer in about twenty midwestern cities. "Why should you buy a new Buick from Ed Houlihan Buick?" he asked. "Because old Ed needs the money, that's why!"

It is not exactly in that spirit that we approach the offering today. There are many more significant reasons for our giving than the church's need for money to carry out its ministries and pay its bills. But to support missionaries, provide materials, underwrite salaries, have a meeting place, and equip a facility, our gifts of money are essential—and it costs more than a little.

That these activities continue is of high importance to us, so we bring prayerfully prepared gifts gladly.

Date Used: _____

General Omar Bradley, with real insight, has said, "Ours is a world of nuclear giants and ethical infants. We know more about war than we know about peace, more about killing than we know about living. We have grasped the mystery of the atom and rejected the Sermon on the Mount."

The church addresses that deficiency with all its strength. Our sacrifices and glad gifts enable the church.

Date Used: _____

Do we need the church? Its message of life in Jesus Christ around here and around the world? Its Sunday school and other programs that teach about eternal things and everyday living? Its class of human friendship? Its resources for grief and crisis? Its worship events? Its reinforcing fellowship? Its atmosphere for thinking and planning and preparing the finest things in life?

Do we need the church?

Our offerings say, "Yes!"

Date Used: _____

Two of today's key ideas are "joy" and "best things." Our giving minutes reflect a part of our "joy" and reflect our determination to take and make available the "best things" to our community and the world community.

Date Used: _____

When someone in the family is sick, you can spend a bundle of money in a very short time. In the past few weeks a lot of money has also been spent making people sick.

Our offerings are given to support a fellowship existing for the purpose of making people well. We give our gifts now to express our commitment to partnership in this enterprise.

Date Used: _____

We give for many reasons. One of the strongest is our desire to reach out with the gospel and with human service. We also make provisions here for worship, fellowship, study, and reinforcement in faith. As we look around at the facilities, we are grateful to faithful Christians of the past generation for foresight and unselfishness. We intend to give the next generation such opportunities, too.

Date Used: _____

Financially we are in an enviable position as a church. This year we will be able to retire a debt, make some large purchases of things we need, and still meet all regular obligations and missionary opportunities. Your generosity is being used in far-flung places. This is a reason for rejoicing together.

Date Used: _____

Wandering around city streets can give one a unique opportunity to observe people. One can watch where they go, hear how they talk, sense where their interests are, see their sadness and emptiness, read their faces. This observation can show one how badly the world needs what Christ can give, and what a frightening world this world would be without the influence of the Lord's church.

Our gifts this morning are calculated to express our strong feeling that what the church seeks to do to make an impact for truth and life is desperately needed.

Date Used: _____

A missionary intern once wrote to her home church to say that she wanted to stay in Rhodesia another six months because she felt more satisfied that she was doing something important for God and her fellow human beings than she had in any work she'd done before.

One reason we bring our gifts today is to make possible that kind of worldwide ministry—witness and service.

Date Used: _____

Several weeks ago a small gang of us went to one house and lifted a beam into place, and then to another and moved a few railroad ties. It was easy! When eight men got under a heavy beam nobody had to lift too much, and we shoved it around like a fat toothpick.

When the tasks and opportunities of the church are enthusiastically, prayerfully, and powerfully shared, great accomplishment will be gained. Our gifts are part of that kind of sharing.

Date Used: _____

During the nation's bicentennial year, one group suggested that at a certain time people join hands in a line all the way across the country. It never happened, but it was a good idea to try to show unity and solidarity. As we bring our prepared offerings we join hands and reach out into the community and around the world. The more of us that join hands, the stronger the impact we have.

Date Used: _____

At some time in recent years you have probably had your car stuck in a ditch, or have helped someone else who was stuck. Five or six of you pushed until you hurt, with no success. Then one more person joined you and you got the car out. One more person pushing can make a real difference. Our regular, thoughtful, devoted offerings undergird the church's ministry and opportunity. And again, one more person pushing makes an important difference.

Date Used: _____

Have you ever heard anyone say, "My church is always asking for money. I wish I could belong to a church that never needed money!"

I'm sure these people don't really mean that. Any church that is alive needs money. Only dead churches do not call on their members for support.

If anyone should accuse your church of always needing and calling for money, regard it as a compliment. Invite this person to rejoice with you that you both belong to a living, growing concern of Jesus Christ rather than a dead, stagnant organization from which the glory of Christ has departed.

—Myron Taylor

Date Used: _____

Thursday morning I sat in the office listening to the birds and smiling at the sunshine finding its way through the thick office windows, and I thought, "Boy, God has given us a nice place." And He wants to give us a nicer one, one that will last forever.

Jesus Christ is the way man gets there, and this church wants to make that fact known to those who haven't heard or haven't cared, and to ingrain the truth more deeply in us all. Your offering today helps to spread that good news.

Date Used: _____

The best and most easily supported institutions in the community are those that do the most good for the most people. If the church is foremost among these, and it certainly should be, then we should want it to go and grow, and readily support what it does.

Date Used: _____

The church is not perfect. We can see several evident flaws because of its human leadership. But the church is incomparably important, and of immeasurable worth.

Our gifts this morning enable the church to stretch, and reach, and speak, and serve; to function in this area as the expression of the body of Christ among men.

Date Used: _____

Recently the stock market took a dramatic upturn. Great news for investors, and a happy thing even for people without any money in the market! It's interesting how that trading floor reacts to the small bit of good news. People want to go with a winner.

The gospel is the "great good news," and the church is the #1 broadcaster. The church has its down moments (because you and I are a part of it, and we are people), but it is divine. The church is a winner! Since we intend to be part of that, we gladly bring our offerings.

Date Used: _____

Giving and Me

Whole-Life
Stewardship

Offering time! Stewardship! Money! How we get, keep, spend, and give are all important parts of our stewardship. But there are other parts too.

We are stewards of the gospel. We anxiously tell people about salvation in Jesus Christ, and welcome them into a fellowship of His servants. Only if we keep quiet will we fail to grow.

We are stewards of our potential. Thousands at our doorstep in this community; people in need of healthy homes and healthy personal lives, people in need of warm Christian fellowship, and people with talent, who, if challenged and channeled for Christ, could give Him great service.

We are stewards of our influence. A strong church, with a strong faith and a firm Bible morality, changes and freshens and strengthens a community.

In all these ways we are stewards of God's gifts.

Date Used: _____

The church keeps on talking about growth, and being larger, and building. Why?

We don't want to grow big just to get the recognition of men. We want to grow in order to serve Jesus Christ better and better, and to gather material and human resources that can be employed to touch thousands of people—even thousands of miles away—for Christ.

Date Used: _____

Times of economic difficulty may have their effect on the church. They may mean making some decisions about what to continue, and keep, and do; and what to stop and slow and maybe even eliminate. It can mean better discipline in our priorities, and that may not really be bad at all, but rather a worthwhile lesson in total stewardship.

A part of that stewardship we express in the gifts we bring now.

Date Used: _____

The government's economic policies are making the front pages these days. Maybe we should think about our own economic policies and the several parts of our stewardship: our getting, our saving, our spending, and our giving. It all counts, to the Christian.

Date Used: _____

Once a young man came to a minister to be baptized. They went to the church building and the minister took off his shoes and opened the baptistery door and told the man to take off his sandals and belt and leave his wallet on the table. "No!" he said. "I want it all to be baptized. Money, too!" and in he walked.

I suppose that is what the offering is all about.

Date Used: _____

I have pledged a loan company twenty-five years of breathtaking payments on a house, and someday soon will have to pledge a few years of car payments. Pledges concerning our money gifts do not bother many of us, either.

Right now let's think about another part of our stewardship. What pledges concerning growth, service, knowledge, Christian maturity, and faithfulness have you and I made to our Lord? Not just cruising through today, but promising for tomorrow.

Date Used: _____

Every now and then I think of the mythical boy angel whose pockets were empty when offering time came, so he carried a basket up before Christ, set it down and plopped himself in. If we offer all we are, the church will never have a financial worry, we will know real joy, and Christ will be

35

properly honored. Paul calls such giving our reasonable service.

Date Used: _____

Stewardship has several parts. It means using everything that comes into our care wisely before God. It means giving with purpose and joy, as we do now. It means directing and using these funds with wisdom to maximize the church's impact. As we give today, shall we pledge to faithfully execute each of these parts of stewardship?

Date Used: _____

The word "stewardship" draws some shudders. "They're beating the drum for money again!" some people complain.

As we grow, we shudder less often and we understand better that good stewardship and Christian living go hand in hand—not just the money we bring right now, and not just how we use this hour. How have we used last week's gift of time? How will we use this week's hours?

Date Used: _____

Offering time gives us a good chance to look carefully at our personal stewardship. How am I using those resources and opportunities that come into my care? Am I handling them in such a way that God can feel free to entrust more resources and more encounters to me? Or am I careless, thoughtless, selfish, squandering, and unaware?

A part of our expression of stewardship is offered now in the bringing of prepared gifts.

Date Used: _____

The Bible is full of examples, exhortation, commands, and warnings about money. Greed is everywhere denounced, and generosity is everywhere extolled. Nor does the Bible contain any apology for its financial emphasis. First Corinthians 15 highlights the resurrection theme: then chapter 16 concerns the collection. Disconcordant? Not really, because it takes resurrection power to get money out of some people! Finances may be the greatest reflection of resurrection reality at work. Everything you possess is sourced in God. It is not what you do with the 10% or 20% you give, but rather what you do with the 80% or 90% you retain.
(From *Heaven Help the Home* by Howard Hendricks, Victor Books.)

Date Used: _____

An old story tells about a cowboy who was converted. He was excited about it and he asked the preacher for the names of ten people who had not been in church for a year so he could write to them. Later he called the preacher. "I thought they would get more attention if I signed your name to them," he said, "so that's what I did."

On Sunday, six of the ten were in church, including the president of First National Bank. After church he caught the preacher and said, "I'll be here every week. I put a tithe in for the year I missed. And by the way, 'Dirty' has only one 't' and there is no 'c' in 'skunk'."

See what excitment for Christ and His church can mean! That excitment is a part of our stewardship.

Date Used: _____

These are some of today's most important minutes. We have a chance to enlarge the offering today and to exercise a bit of stewardship in addition to our carefully prepared money gifts. Give good thinking to the Wednesday evening study classes. A preparing student is an important gift. As the plate goes by think about gifts of time, about more Christlike attitudes, and about a greater readiness to seize opportunities that will honor Christ.

Date Used: _____

It has been said that there really are only two kinds of persons in history—those who want to make the world a better place for everyone, and those who simply want to make a better place for themselves in the world as it is.

Christians are members of the first group, and our giving now takes one step toward affirming that membership.

Date Used: _____

There is more to stewardship of life than just handling money. Just a short word about ultimate stewardship, and a challenge for a week. Do absolutely what you believe you, in the eyes of God and for the good of people, should do—for a day, two days, a week. See how full stewardship feels!

Date Used: _____

Here's a perspective on giving and a thought about priorities from Leonard Griffith, a Canadian minister.

"In 1960, Elvis Presley was paid $125,000 for one night's appearance on a TV program. He did two wiggles and sang two songs and for this received more than the yearly salary of the President of the United States. At the time it was estimated that an identical sum of money would pay the annual salaries of twenty-five schoolteachers, forty-two ministers, or sixty-three farmhands. It would provide a year's training for thirty or more nurses, would give one hundred twenty-five people a year of college, would stock ten mission hospitals with elemental tools and drugs, would feed three thousand refugee children for a whole year."

(From *Illusions of Our Culture* by Leonard Griffith, Word Books Publishers, 1969.)

Every person has his own priorities. You can usually tell what they are by asking three questions about them:

    1) What do you have time for?
    2) How do you spend your wealth?
    3) What do you allow to interrupt you?

Date Used: _____

"Is your local church noted for love, or is it like the parody of 'Onward Christian Soldiers'?

> Like a mighty turtle
>   moves the Church of God;
> Brothers we are treading
>   where we've always trod;
> We are all divided,
>   many factions we;
> Very strong on doctrine,
>   weak on charity.

"If our congregation is going to evangelize our corner of the world, it has to be a unified army of lovers. So you have true doctrine! You have an articulate preacher and a nice building and prospects by the dozen. If you don't have an abundance of love you won't be anything more than a collection of tinkling cymbals and clanging gongs" (Russ Blowers, in a message to the North American Christian Convention).

Channeling God's love to the world is a part of our stewardship too.

Date Used: _____

"Everyone's talking about money!" people complain. "The government thinks it takes more money to run the country, and up go our taxes. Storm window companies won't stop talking when I try to courteously get off the telephone. The Girl Scouts, Heart Fund, Quarterback Club, symphony—where does it all stop? And then there's the church—those folks are not just talking pennies."

It's true! Growth pains have the church talking dollars. But today I want to pass along a perceptive and helpful word from Frances Maitland Balfour about some kinds of giving that Christians will understand. "The best thing to give your enemy is forgiveness; to an opponent, tolerance; to a friend, your heart; to your child, a good example; to your father, deference; to your mother, conduct that will make her proud of you; to yourself, respect; to all people, charity."

The Christian should be doing several good kinds of giving!

Date Used: _____

Sam Stone, in his book, *The Christian Minister,* quotes some lines from an unknown poet that have significance at today's offering time. They talk about our larger stewardship.

You tell what you are by the friends you seek,
By the very manner in which you speak,
By the way you employ your leisure time,
By the use you make of dollar and dime.

You tell what you are by the things you wear,
By the spirit in which your burdens you bear,
By the kind of things at which you laugh,
By the records you play on the phonograph.

You tell what you are by the way you walk,
By the things of which you delight to talk,
By the manner in which you bear defeat,
By so simple a thing as how you eat.

By the books you choose from the well-filled
    shelf;
In these ways, and more, you tell on yourself.

Date Used: _____

The Investment
of Self

Recently I was listening to a tape made by a young person who was reflecting on a year's experience around churches in Germany.

She noted that book members were taxed for the church. They made no personal decision about their commitment of money. They couldn't feel the joy and didn't know the involvement. Her comment was that "They were dead." Sure!

Today's gladly given gifts are an expression of our life.

Date Used: _____

Most community fund drives have gotten a smile and a dollar from this preacher—when they can catch me.

But one time several years ago now, I was asked to be chairman of the county Red Cross drive, and I promptly kicked in ten dollars. Why was that? It seemed natural. I was a part of it.

That's one reason why our giving for the life of the church is vital. It reminds us that we are partners in the church's enterprise, and that's what God wants and deserves.

Date Used: _____

One church used a questionnaire in its approach to underwriting the regular budget. The questionnaire asked each family's gross income and issued a statement as to how much that family would be expected to give.

We really get our backs up at that.

What's the problem? Asking too much? No, several families here give more than the church officials would ever ask. Is it none of their business? Not exactly! Spiritual growth is the business of leaders, and nothing demonstrates growth better than giving.

The problem is that a rich experience in giving can never be dictated by someone else. We do it with determination and love, and we are blessed beyond measure.

Date Used: _____

On vacation we visited one of the great churches in the midwest, and before the service started the young couple behind us leaned up to say, "Welcome to our church." It was a glad expression of their investment. However long they had been members, they had learned to say "our" church.

Date Used: _____

A significant change in Christian maturity happens when we move from saying "Why doesn't somebody do that?" or "Why don't you do that?" to "Why don't I do that?"

Our giving pattern, as we grow, takes just the same course.

Date Used: _____

Wouldn't it be nice if the Lord's work could be done without money? We wouldn't have to worry about offerings, drives, paying for buildings, or supporting local and world ministries.

No, it wouldn't!

Jesus talked more about our use of things than He did about anything else. How we handle our getting, keeping, and giving is all-important. In the dedicated giving we do now, we are able to be part of a great undertaking—sounding, sending, and growing in the gospel.

Date Used: _____

This past week a great crew cleaned this whole building; they gave a lot of time, effort, and love. Now, this morning, this group will hold back their gifts a bit, won't they? They've done their part. The offerings are up to the rest of us!

No, it just doesn't work that way. The group that did the cleaning will still carry a big chunk of the financial load. They love the Lord and this fellowship, and this is another way they find to show it.

Date Used: _____

John Knox wrote about the reply of Jesus to the man who asked Him to make a brother divide an inheritance with him. Jesus wouldn't do it! Then Knox used a phrase. "God does not hear our complaints against others," Knox wrote, "He asks, 'What about you?'"

In the blessings and expectations concerning a Christian's giving, each of us should ask, "What about me?"

Date Used: _____

We bring our gifts, and more than that—we bring ourselves. "To think that God can change the world by using individuals is idealistic, but to think that he will do it without individuals is idiotic." (Weatherhead)

Think about it—Christ can change some part of the world by using me!

Date Used: _____

"You are the salt of the earth." Salt is known for its usefulness.

In the days when one started work with as little

as two shillings a week, a boy got his first pay and gave it to his mother. The next day he and his family sat at the evening meal. On the table there was a loaf still uncut, and his mother took the loaf and began to slice it. "Johnny," she said, looking up, "it was you who bought this loaf for us."

That was her way of telling him he had become a real contributor to the family. And even though he later became wealthy and famous, he never again had a moment that made him feel as proud.

We are proud, too, to be useful!

Date Used: _____

The country of Sweden is officially Lutheran, with all Swedes considered members of the church. Only 3% or so are in church most Sundays. In some parishes not one person shows up for Sunday service. Per capita giving is about $1.50 a year.

There are a lot of reasons for such lack of support—first, people believe "the church doesn't need me" (my presence, my insights, my support, my fellowship). Second, the church more often is a battleground of controversy rather than an arena of faith, truth, and real love.

God has given. He offers life through Christ. He has ordained the church and it needs me. Here we shall not fight but love, teach, and believe. My gifts are a part of me, and I believe in Christ's church.

Date Used: _____

It's healthy to examine regularly our level of giving—and not just to meet the church's growth needs. A plain fact of life is that our interest follows our financial involvement. As the size of the gift increases our concern for the church's welfare, its plans, its outreach, and its function increases. That's what we want to see! Think about giving more, and we can count on you for partnership at the core of Christ's church.

Date Used: _____

Some of you gladly give quite a good-sized offering each week. Multiply that times fifty-two sometime—WOW! That's ten suits and dresses! That's a small car! More than an annual fuel bill! More than my income tax! Two weeks' vacation!

That's a lot of money! Isn't it great joy to know that you have dedicated this to Christ's kingdom—the business of eternity?

Date Used: _____

"It's only money!"
"What's it for if not to use?"
You and I say those things and they're true! Today's offering is our expression of a determination to *use* an important part of what we get for the King's business.

Date Used: _____

You may be a small-time investor like I am! I enjoy it. If I bought some Standex stock, I would care quite a bit how smoothly the presses of Standard Publishing run. If I invested in the oil supplies on the north slopes being developed by Phillips Petroleum, I would be very interested in how the local 66 station was doing. I've had a bond for the campus ministry at our university. My donations have increased so that they might pay off their bonds. My gifts to the Lord's business are an investment that assures my concern about how the work of the kindgom of God goes among men. All of me cares!

Date Used: _____

I look at the stack of bills, checks and scattered coins on the desk in front of me—our collection for the mission fund. It doesn't look like ordinary money to me. It is actually minted human life and sacrifice. Not many come by money easily. It represents "blood, sweat, and tears."

I picture a working man with a family. He is a Christian. He knows the church has needs, and that God expects some return for the blessings He has bestowed upon him.

Out of his wallet he selects a $20 bill, smooths it, folds it and sets it aside for the church. He needs a new pair of shoes, but patiently he picks up his badly worn ones and takes them to the shoe shop for repair. They will do for another six months.

I picture the mother of a large family. She is wondering how much they can afford to give to the mission fund. She casts a worried glance at the worn living room carpet. Well, maybe by placing an inexpensive scatter rug in front of the fireplace, and another in front of the davenport, she can cover the worn spots and get by for another year.

What is this currency in front of me? Money? Human sacrifice? What is it in the eyes of God?

There seemed to be a gentle fragrance about me. This is it. The money is really flowers—heavenly flowers of unearthly fragrance.

Gently I began to lift each bill as I counted. These were the most fragrant of all flowers.

As I relaxed at home that night, I hugged to my heart a secret joy. Some of the fragrance of those flowers, given with sacrifice by God's own true flock, still clung to me.

—Marjorie Grant in *The Elyria* (Ohio) *Messenger*

Date Used: _____

Have you ever asked yourself as you put the envelope in the plate, "What does this mean?"

For many it means, "I love Christ, His church, the people that this will touch, and the growth that it can promote. Boy, what a privilege and joy to be able to do this."

Or does it mean, "not much. It's the thing to do. I'm paying my dues. It's a token of my membership." As long as that is what I think, the church is never going to do me much good.

Several of our gifts say, "A lot of other things are more important, and they come first. The church is an afterthought, a minor thing."

The most important things in our lives should have the most prominent attention in our checkbooks. "Where you money is, there your heart is." And where should our hearts be?

Date Used: _____

A Reflection of Self

Thomas Carlyle said, "Make yourself an honest man, and then you may be sure there is one rascal less in the world." His statement speaks to our stewardship of our lives and to our stewardship of giving. Our contribution is extremely important, and should be our primary personal concern.

Date Used: _____

I was mildly surprised to hear some of the ticket prices for the winter Olympic games—$22 for hockey, $39 for downhill skiing, $56 for pairs figure skating. But I guess if the Olympic games are really important, that's okay.

We seem to fairly readily pay what we need to spend if we eat out—$6 for two at the nearest fast-food restaurant, $30 for steak dinners, or $60 for a nice meal at one of those French places. But I guess if fine dining is important, that's okay.

How important is the mission of the church of the Son of God?

Date Used: _____

I heard about a fly that landed on a strip of flypaper and said, "My flypaper." But the flypaper said, "My fly."

That story has a moral. That's exactly what can happen as we handle our possessions. "Our possessions" we say. But sometimes the possessions could properly say, "My family."

Unless we *really* have control of them, they do indeed have control of us. As we give an important chunk of what we have and get, we indicate that we do have control, and choose to turn it loose for the vital purposes of Christ's church.

Date Used: _____

On an island off the west coast of Florida, hotel rooms start at $150 a night, houses sell for $400,000 and condominiums the same; there are beautiful boats and golf courses, and all kinds of stuff— quite a treasure for those who own it all.

I wonder what churches those people are causing to thrive and bear a great witness, what missionary ventures they back, what hurting humans they help? "Lay not up for yourselves treasure on earth."

Date Used: _____

What institutions would thrive in the world if my pattern of life were multiplied by the number of people in the community? Gas stations would thrive even more; there would be a chili parlor every three blocks; every distillery and brewery shut down; clothing stores would have a lot of lookers.

What would the church be like, we might ask ourselves, if what I do and give were multiplied by the number of people who are part of it? Would it founder and die? Or would it multiply its service and impact many times?

Date Used: _____

When we're spending, we have an excellent opportunity to consider our giving—car repair, lawn mower, insurance, school clothes, vacation, picnic, and more. What are the most important things? Our offerings help spell that out!

Date Used: _____

You have heard the phrase, "Money talks!" Our offerings today talk, too: they say, (1) "Thank you, God!" (2) "Long live the church!" (3) "We care!" (4) "Here I am!" (5) "I believe!"

Date Used: _____

My Financial Commitment

1. Does it adequately reflect my love for Christ?
2. Does it exceed the tithe (10% of my income)?
3. Does its size require faith on my part to do it?
4. Would Jesus be pleased with me?
5. If God used it alone to determine my gratitude to Him, would it pass the test?
6. Is it more than I'll spend on skiing, games, boating, vacation, and self-entertainment?
7. Could the world look at it and determine by it that I'm truly one of Christ's disciples?
8. Does it reflect my concern for world missions?

Date Used: _____

W.A. Criswell tells a story about attending an Oklahoma-Texas football game. One Oklahoma fan on the Texas side stood up, and waved a $100 bill. "I'll give seven points!" he said. No takers! Still later he said, "I'll give twenty-one points!"

"I wish that man was a member of my church,"

Criswell said. "He's enthusiastically behind his team, and he puts his money where his mouth is."

Date Used: _____

The neighbors in our community think this is really a rich church—our building, our missions program, our staff members, our strong regular offerings. We *are* rich, but not the way they think. We're just working folks who love the Lord and delight in His church. We want it to be a great one, and to do as much for the Christ as we possibly can.

It's time for us rich folks to bring our prepared offering.

Date Used: _____

"There is a quaint Scotch story of a certain penurious lord of Fife, whose weekly contributions to the church never exceeded the sum of one penny. Yet he was immensely rich. It was the custom in that church to drop one's offering in the plate that was held at the door as one passed into the sanctuary for worship. One Sunday, by mistake, he dropped a five-shilling piece. Discovering his error before he was seated in his pew, he hurried back. He was just about to replace the silver piece with his usual penny when the elder who kept watch over the plate challenged him, 'Stop, my lord,' said he. 'Ye may put what ye like in, but ye must not take anything out.' After some discussion, in which the elder turned a deaf ear to the wealthy man's plea, the latter said, 'Aweel, I suppose I'll get credut fie ut in heaven.' 'No, no,' said the elder. 'Ye'll only get credut fir the penny.' And he was right. The manner in which the contribution was made marred the whole procedure and discounted the value of what was given."

(From *Meet Yourself in the Bible* by Roy L. Laurin. Copyright ©Mrs. Marian Laurin. Moody Press, 1970.)

Date Used: _____

Maybe we are short on gas, or maybe the oil companies are holding it back. Whichever the case, gas prices remain high. But the American people are a surprise; they drive anyway. They burn gas and go where they want to go. What we love we support. And we love our vacations and our cars and our "going." We may gripe, but we fill up the tank.

We love our Lord and His church, and bring our gladly prepared gifts now.

Date Used: _____

The average Protestant gives five cents a week to foreign missions. He is that excited about world community in the name of Christ. According to this year's average attendance, we give _____ a week each. It's a good time to ask ourselves what we are excited about. If we follow where our resources go, we will get a pretty clear picture.

Date Used: _____

Someone said, "Show me a man's checkbook and I can write his biography." Add his credit cards to that, and watch him spend cash for a few days, and you could get a pretty accurate picture of what he's like.

The Scripture talks about the heart being where the treasure is. Our gifts this morning are a graphic illustration of our affections and investments. The Lord loves you cheerful givers.

Date Used: _____

Benefits of Giving

"Tithing makes me feel so rich," said one mother as she was writing checks to the church and to mission organizations. "We have all this money to give away."

That's right! Many of us have learned that kind of joy. But some can't understand. They don't know the feeling. Too bad!

Date Used: _____

At offering time we think a variety of things, positive things, many of us. That's why the bright, moving music we often hear at offering time is so right. Sometimes we remember challenging reminders too, like a comment from Fred Smith, Christian financier from Dallas, Texas: "Many of us are dwarfed in our spiritual lives by our refusal to give, because our money is where our ego is located. Giving is the drainplug for our greed."

Date Used: _____

Someone in the city this week won $100. Someone else gave $100. I wonder who will have the joy longer?

Date Used: _____

Yesterday I was thinking of some of my happiest times . . . filled with pure joy, rich experience; the times of spiritual fulfillment. Many are associated with giving—gifts to family and friends; unexpected little things. Preparing to give to the Lord's business is still a thrill, too . . . and it is more. In the process of facing spiritual opportunity, we meet a strong personal need.

Date Used: _____

Miami electrical engineer Hugh McNatt, 43, has dropped the suit he filed against his church, 4,200-member Allapattah Baptist. In his suit he had charged that God, contrary to what Pastor Donald Manuel of Allapattah had promised, did not bestow blessings and rewards for his $800 tithe given three years before. McNatt dropped the suit after getting his $800 back (without interest). A San Antonio businessman, Alton S. Newell, read a news story about the case and decided to repay on behalf of the church. Newell is a member of San Antonio's First Baptist Church.

Tangible rewards are not always coming in return for our gifts, and usually when they do come it is when we don't particularly care about rewards. Be sure that God does reward the cheerful giver, though, in many ways.

Date Used: _____

In moments of frustration when Sunday's offering doesn't come together easily, we think, "Wouldn't it be nice if we had a couple millionaires in the church who could just underwrite the budget?" Then we remember quickly that we would be robbed of the blessing of being vitally important partners in the business of the kingdom of God.

Date Used: _____

One wealthy man heard that God always returned more then He got, so he started giving more handsomely in order that he might get more in return.

Sometimes God does give back coins; sometimes He gives other things. But gifts tainted with pride and selfishness He will not honor. We give because it is our privilege that God has put important things in our hands. We intend to handle those things for Him. We know that hoarded possessions represent a sickness unto death.

Date Used: _____

Money is a sensitive subject. It seems hard to get, easy to get rid of, exciting to spend, and almost impossible to save. Usually the bills amount to just a little more than is available. Yet, for us, giving is one of the most enjoyable things we do. As we give, now, we can watch our money cover a lot of territory and meet a variety of needs.

Date Used: _____

We can begin to get a little bit excited about giving when we ask, "What and whom will my gift benefit most this week?" And answer, "Me."

Date Used: _____

A Florida church has solved the problem of how to get people to come to church. The church will issue green trading stamps to all who attend services. At every meeting, eager worshipers may be seen pasting their newly acquired stickers into the cherished book of stamps. As the minister preaches, some parishioners will be dreaming of new electric roasters, golf clubs, and fancy new storm doors. Others will be calculating how many more Sundays they'll have to attend before getting enough stamps for an outboard motor.

Peter, at the pearly gate, is going to be mighty confused when someone says, "But you have to let me in—I've got six and three-fifths books."

Nothing we do is so frivolous. We have not been beguiled into coming! We attend because being here gives us strength.

Date Used: _____

Why didn't God design the support system of the church in such a way that the needs for growth and service might be met from the divine wealth, without the need for this offering time? Because that would cheat *us*! You have seen a few children to whom everything was given and who gave nothing. A loving God doesn't want that stale and worthless condition to happen to us.

Date Used: _____

In 1 Kings there is a curious story about Elijah the prophet. He came to a widow's house and asked for a bit of refreshment. All she had was a tiny handful of meal with which she was going to make a little cake to split with her starving son. "But I'll make it for you," she said. And he let her.

How selfish! Can that really be God's prophet?

But then we see why. When the widow exercised that splendid grace of total giving, the bowl of flour and jar of oil were filled. Even as the widow and her son used the flour and oil, they stayed full as long as the famine lasted.

Date Used: _____

Some people, a little slow of mind, shout "Give me what I deserve!" I don't want what I deserve! But with great joy I accept the grace of God that gives so much more.

Neither do we bring our offerings this morning to give to the business of God what He deserves. We can't give that much! But it is also with great joy that we give back a part.

Date Used: _____

"Congregations have personalities too. Some are warm, expansive, generous, and joyful. They attract us. Others resemble Scrooge, and we avoid them.

"Generous churches make their plans according to what they believe God wants them to do, not according to what they can afford.

"Much more could be added, but these observations prove that the members of such congregations put *people* values ahead of *money* values, the kingdom of God above the kingdom of Mammon. Where people matter, the church rings with laughter and holds together in mutual acceptance and encouragement. Such churches cannot help growing. Generous people attract others." (LeRoy Lawson, "Reflections," *Christian Standard,* November 9, 1980.)

Date Used: _____

Lyman Beecher had been laid up for some time with a serious illness when Mr. Fithian, hateful and stingy, threatened to stop paying Beecher. "What is the reason," the wretched old man asked, "you ministers are so hungry for money?"

But the Puritan firebrand was ready for him. "I don't know," he replied, "unless it is that we see our people growing covetous and going to hell, and want to get it away from them."

Date Used: _____

Proverbs 11:24, 25 says, "There is one who scatters, yet increases all the more, and there is one who withholds what is justly due, but it results only in want. The generous man will be prosperous, and he who waters will himself be watered" (NASB).

I don't know how God works this out, but it is true. We do not give to gain, but the one who has a giver's heart has a gainer's blessings. And the one who holds back more than is really needed for himself and his, soon has empty hands.

Jesus didn't talk about giving as much as He did because he wanted to corner the things people had. He talked about a spirit that we desperately need, personally, to get by giving.

Date Used: _____

Faith and Giving

The non-Christian life is a life controlled by desire. And those desires are never satisfied. Lust is in control—the lust of the eyes (materialism), the lust of the flesh (immorality), and the pride of life (self-centered importance) (1 John 2:16).

The antidote is to learn and practice giving.

Date Used: _____

There are two approaches to looking at the tasks of the church involving financing. 1) We could say, "How can we ever?" and be careful not to move too fast or reach too far; 2) We could say, "How can we not?" and launch out to do those things that will glorify the kingdom of God.

When a church becomes committed to what God wants, it seldom has to retrench. Let's ask, "Does God want it?" and if the answer is "Yes," let's do it.

Date Used: _____

Why should we give money to save the heathen abroad when there are heathen at home? Why should I give money to those in other parts of the country when there are needy right in my own state? Why should I give to the poor in the town when my own church needs money? Why should I give to the church when my own family needs the money? Why should I give to my family when I can use it myself?

Why? Because I am a Christian and not a heathen.

Date Used: _____

A recent *Wall Street Journal* had an interesting article about unfulfilled executives with substantial incomes who left their work and entered seminaries to prepare for the ministry. One took $100,000 in personal savings and supported himself and the family (including two sons in college) while he finished that work.

"It was all worthwhile," he said, "We live in a security minded society. Dynamic life comes only when you step out in faith."

Faith, not security, is the door to dynamic life. The days just ahead will give us all the chance to venture, with vision and refreshing faith. None of us will want to miss the chance. Today's gifts are a small expression of that energy—that faith.

Date Used: _____

Responsibility

Have you worked a jigsaw puzzle recently? Each piece is unique; no two pieces will really fit in the same place. Without every piece the puzzle is incomplete. But when each piece is slotted in the right place, they often make up an amazingly lovely picture.

Giving time offers us one reminder of the vital importance of each piece—each member of the family. Each one of us makes our contribution to the picture! Each one of us is really important! And the church is incomplete, and not so lovely, if we fail in our part.

Each of us should ask right now, "Am I filling my slot? In what ways can I make a fuller contribution?" One way comes in the sharing of that part of our family's life that is expressed in these commitments of money.

Date Used: _____

Our Sunday morning Bible School is growing wonderfully. Our Sunday evening youth activities are exciting and valuable. Our worship attendances have outstretched our largest hopes. People are growing and the church is growing. It looks as though we have a large, important place to fill tomorrow. Unless we also grow in earnest, happy, and significant giving, some opportunities will have to wait.

The "we" of this church ripples with potential. What will *we* do?

Date Used: _____

Jamie Buckingham writes, "All the holy men seem to have gone off and died. There's no one left but us sinners to carry on the ministry."

That's the way it is. There will be less sin and more Christ as we grow. But the ministry is ours. We are unfinished, challenged, and privileged.

We bring glad gifts because the kingdom ministry is in our hands.

Date Used: _____

An amazing and distressing thing about conventions is the degree of private conversation that goes on during the music, features, and even preaching. Apparently 500 people all think that one conversation won't make any difference among 12,000. How great it could be if *everyone* were involved in the singing and the listening and the praying!

Offering time expresses that everybodiness—a pulling together in powerful unity, for a great church, to the glory of God.

Date Used: _____

In California, prison inmates have the right to sue the state for worker's compensation and other benefits. Recently a robber sued his victims for shooting and wounding him. Arrested suspects regularly sue the arresting officers for brutality. And now children are successfully suing their parents for additional money for "education." Judges are awarding children money for education in keeping with the economic status of the family. But what really makes us feel secure that our rights are being adequately defended is the suit of a

Houston, Texas man who injured himself while sliding into a second base on a city-owned softball field. He is suing the city for using "second-class" dirt on their softball fields.

Whatever happened to "every man shall bear his own burden" (Galatians 6:5)? Is it any wonder we have to have more and more rules to govern every aspect of our life? No one is responsible for himself. It is someone else's responsibility.

Date Used: _____

The reason for offering meditations is to stimulate us to think about the joy and opportunity of making offering time an important expression of dedication.

My problem may be how to communicate these truths to the ones who would benefit most from growth in this matter.

Often those who hear most are those who are already most sensitive to the call and blessings of giving—and may do better about it than I do.

Maybe I'm the next best candidate for the lesson, or maybe you are. We'll be blessed if we learn.

Date Used: _____

Money talks.
More than one-half million fewer households

watched the ABC network one November than during the previous nine weeks, according to figures released by the A.C. Nielsen Company. Donald E. Wildmon, Executive Director of the National Federation for Decency, was elated by the figures. He attributed the drop—which he says will cost the network millions of dollars in advertising revenues—to a November boycott of the network that was planned by his group to protest sex, violence, and profanity in programming.

Date Used: _____

It's not what you'd do with a million
    If a million were your lot
It's what you are doing at present
    With the dollar and a quarter you've got.

Date Used: _____

There are two basic approaches to our giving. One pays bills, plans outings, buys things, and on Sunday morning says. "Now what's left to give?" The other happily lays aside a gift for God and then turns to the papers and the plans and says, "Now what's left?"

Date Used: _____

I have a friend who doesn't tip waitresses. "They make almost as much as I do, anyway," she reasons. "And all those businessmen on expense accounts and people who have more money will make up for my part." That reasoning may have some merit.

Sometimes, though, that's the mentality of the church. "The wealthy people can afford to give better than I can. They can give out of their surplus and make up for the little I might contribute."

But so few ever feel wealthy enough to have an easily tappable surplus. Most of us dream of things we would do and have if we made more.

The truth is that if we will not tithe a little, we would not tithe if we had a lot. And another truth is that we need to give. We will not have a blessed and intimate association with the purposes of God unless we do. We have some pleasant surprises coming as we return to God His part of our insufficient incomes.

Date Used: _____

Growth

Givers generally come in three categories: in which are you?

The infant Christian does not give to anyone—

or maybe to those who threaten, or those who promise greater reward. He gives for self-protection and with thinly veiled self interest.

The more grown-up Christian gives in response to external pleas. When a need can be spelled out and a proper emotional atmosphere set, he will gladly give.

The mature Christian gives in response to internal urgings and as a result of personal decision, determination, and love. Such giving includes that which we do as the church.

Date Used: _____

It is no mistake that "miser" and "miserable" sound suspiciously alike. And it is absolutely true that giving and a joyous spirit are constant companions.

We give because the work the church does ought to be done among men, and because God expects back a portion of what He has given us. But we also give because of the great personal need we have for the development that the spirit of giving brings.

Date Used: _____

If we increase our income more than the current rate of inflation, we rejoice at having moved forward. It we do not increase at that pace, but learn to adjust painlessly to the lower standard, we have been successful too.

We flinch at soaring grocery prices, gasoline costs, and other energy bills, and more. But has our giving inflated with income and costs, or have we felt that somehow the tasks of the church are joyously exempt from any of that?

Date Used: _____

Some of the people in our church give regularly, heavily, and readily for its program and outreach. Others give very little. Have you wondered what the difference is?

"They have it to give. They're wealthier," say the ones who give little.

That's not it at all. Those whose giving is the strongest are completely ordinary. It's a matter of their priorities, dedication, vision, and affection.

Date Used: _____

Several small Christian colleges are climbing out of debt; several new congregations need to put up buildings. I'm sure that any of these places would be glad to help use up any offering surpluses we might have.

If we grow in our giving to the place where sharing is best for us, we will be able to help meet growing building needs and share with missions, schools, and sister churches. That sharing will then add to our blessings even more.

Date Used: _____

I am a dollar.
   I am not on speaking terms with the butcher;
   I am unable to buy a gallon of gasoline;
   I am small change at the supermarket;
   I am too little to go the the movies by myself;
   I am hardly even big enough for a decent tip.
   But when I go to church on Sunday, I am considered SOME MONEY.

Date Used: _____

We've heard a lot of exciting talk around here lately, about building expansion, missions chal-lenges, and expansion of our youth and music programs. But it's going to take the dedication of our financial resources to stay on the grow, as the Lord deserves. Our giving has been very good. Exciting new commitments have been made.
   Let's just keep growing. Great things will happen.

Date Used: _____

Our congregation has been determined from the beginning to make a difference—a difference for Christ in the community, for the benefit of the people it touches. We are determined to be great!

What is it that will make this family great?

1) What we get from God—strength and joy and peace—that comes when His people surrender to His Son as Lord!

2) The love and fellowship that members of the family get from each other.

3) What we get from ourselves, because spiritual insight puts our lives in order. We increasingly less often violate ourselves, confuse ourselves. We are prepared for handling prosperity.

4) What we get from the meaningful, happy experiences of worship and study we share here.

We can be great because of what we get, and from an awakened faith.

But more, this family will be great because of what we give—to God (real worship), to brethren, to a world with massive needs. Today's offering is a good opportunity for us to express greatness. We are determined to give to missionary partners in other places, to schools that train leaders for the church, to new churches, and to occasions for rich Christian fellowship.

This family will become increasingly great as we rejoice in our giving.

Date Used: _____

Someone once said that you like the people best to whom you are allowed to give. Our giving brings us closer to our children, parents, friends, and people with needs to whom we respond.

"For God so loved . . . that He gave. . ." It may be that God challenges us to be the way His church reaches forward, so that through our giving we might be drawn closer to Him.

Date Used: _____

Our giving ought to be a family affair. It would make a good family devotional experience to talk about how and why we give our gifts to the church. How do we determine what to give? Other family members may have some fine contributions to make to the discussion and plans.

Date Used: _____

I haven't examined the list of givers to this church, and I don't intend to. Whether already diligent stewards have muscled up and are carrying bigger loads, or new Christians are bringing their first sacrificial gifts, or 200 of us have gladly added one dollar or five dollars, I don't know. But the Lord knows!

New opportunities are opening up for local impact, for building to welcome growth, for benevolence, and for world outreach that we are only beginning to imagine.

Date Used: _____

Sometimes we give and don't get much recognition or credit. That doesn't bother us. In fact, there is often increased satisfaction in careful giving done secretly.

Sometimes we give and it is misunderstood. Love can get us in trouble with people who attribute the world's motives to things Christians do. But we will continue to give, and serve, and grow, and serve, and grow. . . . God always understands the real motives.

Date Used: _____

The church's finances have had a very good year. Our obligations have been steadily met, debt responsibility shaved, programs and materials made readily available through your dedicated dollars, and our missionary outreach is finer than ever before. The church's Groom is glad.

Date Used: _____

One man who was originally opposed to his church's faith-promise missions program later turned around and committed $400 a week—half of his income.

Would we do that? What have we done with smaller amounts?

Date Used: _____

As boys our neighborhood gang needed to collect money to buy a basketball, so we carefully divided out how much each fellow would have to raise. "I've done my part," each one said. "Where's yours?"

Not long ago a group of men were collecting travel expenses for a visiting speaker. No one worried about quotas, or what the other man chipped in. "What's left over, we'll give to the camp," they said. "They can use it."

As our faith in Christ and love for His church grows, that's what happens here. We may start by asking, "How much do we have to make up?" Later we move to, "We'll give, and pray that there is extra left for spreading the gospel and Christ's kindness even further."

Date Used: _____

Since the last board meeting, I have been thinking about spaghetti pots. Two of these and other assorted pans have evaporated from the kitchen, and the kitchen committee would be delighted if they came back home. Don't put them in the trays this morning!

Wouldn't it be something if we needed spaghetti pots to take up the Sunday offering? What we could do for Christian education, for benevolence in the name of Christ, for world evangelism, for retiring building debts, for launching new ones, and so much more as a kingdom honoring Christ!

If we prepare and give aggressively and with a spark in our eye, maybe we'll need spaghetti pots.

Date Used: _____

Vision will always be carried by a few! In the church those few will give more, work more, love more, and win more—and be blessed more, in every conceivable way—than the big group gathered at the edge of the church.

I hope that we few—all of us—from today forward will be more fiercely committed to moving this church to the greatness of the servant of all, Jesus Christ.

Date Used: _____

Just a few days ago I heard a fellow say, "I'm giving more and loving it more!'

Do you think he was kind of odd? Not at all! That's the witness of many growing Christians. As I live more of the lifestyle of Jesus Christ, I will enjoy it more.

Date Used: _____

Sometimes at camp, one can see parables on Christian maturity. One young fellow spent most of his money in the camp canteen, dropped a little change in the missionary offering, and counted out seven dollar bills to take home. One girl was sitting at the table on Friday when the camp pictures were passed out. She had put ten dollars in the missionary offering, and didn't have the money to buy a picture. But she didn't mind.

These two kids enacted a parable about the tight fisted and the open handed—the grim and the happy.

Date Used: _____

This week has given me several occasions to praise God for another kind of offering many of you are making—the offering of committed Christian growth and maturity of spirit.

Some of you are able to turn crisis into victory. Others can absorb unthoughtfulness and offer kindness in return. Others are learning to appreciate even very different people who love and want to serve the Lord. You are studying, serving, and gaining self control. I thank God for your gifts.

Date Used: _____

The Art of Giving

The Tithe

There is one talent we all seem to have. We seem to be able to spend whatever we make. If we make $10,000 we live on that. If we make $20,000 we live on that. The same is true for $50,000, I guess.

It is also true that if circumstance cuts us back, we manage to adjust and live on what is available.

Hundreds of thousands of people have proven that they live just as well on what is left after God gets His proper part of what comes into their hands. That is both a psychological reality and a divine provision.

If you haven't tried it, go ahead. You have a pleasant surprise coming. The kingdom work surges forward, and you will be better off indeed.

Date Used: _____

When I went to college, it cost $1,000 a year, everything included. When I was first married, we spend $10 a week on groceries, without coupons.

Of course, in my first full-time church I made $4,579.64 a year; our tithe was about $9 a week.

Prices have changed, too. That's one thing we need to think about, for our health, and the serving family of the church.

Date Used: _____

Sometimes I wonder why God came up with one tenth as an appropriate amount of their income for His people to return to Him. Why not one twentieth, or one fifth?

God designated one of the twelve tribes of Israel as priests. They were to serve and be supported by the other tribes, and there were probably some expenses involved in maintaining the synagogue and temple—so one tenth comes out pretty close.

Whatever the reason, God has suggested that this portion qualifies as solid giving, and as a fitting place for great giving to begin. And since He has given us everything we have, that seems more than fair.

Date Used: _____

One man in the medical profession had been a nominal Christian until his faith caught fire. Then he wanted to do the right thing with his money, so he started giving a tithe of his income to the church (a healthy amount, over $100 a week).

His wife worried, "People will think you're showing off."

"Not many people will know," he said. "But for my sake, I have to do it even if they find out!"

Few of us face that problem, but we do know that we give because giving is important to us.

Date Used: _____

When the man at the savings and loan figured up how much they could lend for our home mortgage, one question he failed to ask was "How much do you give to the church?" Either he didn't know that he had only 90% of our income to work with, or he *did* know that people who have tithing built into their lifestyle handle the payments as well as anyone. Strange, but true!

Date Used: _____

An acquaintance was talking about tithing, and his quick conclusion was that anyone who gave 10% of his income to the church was ready for the little padded wagon to be backed up to his door.

But this *whole business* of the Christian faith strikes the world as foolish. "The foolishness of God is wiser than men, and the weakness of God is stronger than men" (1 Corinthians 1:25).

The careful giver is right in step . . . not with all the world, but with God.

Date Used: _____

It is true that God makes the tither's 90% go farther than his whole income would—but why? Perhaps because the satisfaction that comes to the Christian makes unnecessary a lot of the things people think they need to be happy. The peace, assurance, and sense of purpose the Christian has makes expensive flings or searching for some kind of satisfaction unnecessary.

God always gives us more than we give Him.

Date Used: _____

Today we are going to talk about freedom! That concept is involved in the giving of our gifts, too! The elders have not come to your door to tell you just how much you must give. God has given us a guideline in the Old Testament that has, properly, been adopted by many Christians: a tithe, ten percent. But in the spirit of freedom we rejoice that a *ceiling* has not been put on what we may give. As we grow we can give more of our time, resources, witness, and affections.

Date Used: _____

When the six-year-old son of a Texan pledged $100 a week to the church, the preacher, feeling the boy did not know what he was doing, called on his parents.

"It's perfectly in order," the father assured him. "We insist that the boy tithe!"

Date Used: _____

Did you know that Christians almost always have more money than non-Christians making the same income? The Christian is no longer ruled by himself, or by the gadgets that are thought necessary to make an unfulfilled self happy. The big sums that poor souls spend to indulge themselves, the Christians has for family, for helpful possessions, and for gladly supporting his part of the work of Christ's kingdom.

You have heard that 90% with Christ is more than 100% without Him. It's really true!

Date Used: _____

Years ago a young man knelt with his preacher as he committed himself to give a tenth of what he earned to the Lord. His first week's pay was $10 and the tenth was $1. As he grew older he became more prosperous, and his tenth was $7.50 a week, then $10.00. He moved to another city and soon his tenth was $100. Then it grew to $200 per week.

He sent for the preacher. The preacher arrived at the man's beautiful home and they had a good time talking over old times. Finally, the man came to the point. "You remember the promise of the tenth that I made years ago? How can I be released?" When he first made the promise, the man said, he only had to give a dollar. But now he had to give $500 per week, and he couldn't afford to go around giving money away on that scale.

The old preacher looked at his friend and said, "I'm afraid we cannot get a release from that promise but we can kneel here and ask God to shrink your income so you can afford to give a dollar again."

Would you want God to shrink your income so that your present giving would be a tenth?

Date Used: _____

The white frame Church of Christ in West Mansfield, Ohio, has a new foundation, roof, baptistery, kitchen, carpet, sidewalk, bulletin board, and church bus, plus an assistant pastor, all made possible by a race horse named Rambling Willie.

Willie is half-owned by Vivian Farrington, daughter of the church's pastor, C. Lloyd Harris, age 85. Harris brought his daughter up to believe in tithing, and she gives ten percent of Willie's winnings to the church. The eight-year-old horse virtually came out of nowhere to win more than $1 million so far. Tithes on his winnings last year exceeded $50,000.

Mrs. Farrington's husband bought a half-interest in the horse in 1973 for $15,000 and gave it to her for a birthday present. Until then Willie had won no races.

"The Lord said to give ten percent and He would bless you," Mrs. Farrington told a reporter. "So when my husband gave the horse to me, I said I would tithe, and the Lord sure provided like He says."

When we are faithful to our part, the Lord will

bless, indeed—and He sometimes blesses in strange ways. If it is He who is spurring Willie across the finish line, so be it.

Date Used: _____

The treasurer of a church resigned. The elders asked another to take his position, the man who managed the grain elevator. He agreed under two conditions: (1) That no report from the treasurer be necessary for a year, and (2) that no one ask him any questions about the church's finances during this period of time.

The elders gulped, but finally agreed, since he was a trusted man in the community and well known to most of them because they did business with him as manager of the local grain elevator.

At the year's end he reported: "The indebtedness of $25,000 on the church building has been paid in full. The church parsonage has been redecorated, the minister's salary substantially increased, the church's missions quota paid 200 percent. There are no outstanding bills, and the cash balance in the treasury is $12,523.46."

Immediately the shocked congregation asked, "How did you do it?"

"I didn't," he said. *"You did.*

"Most of you men bring your grain to my elevator. As you did business with me, I simply withheld ten percent of your profit on your behalf. You never even missed it! What you then gave on

Sunday was your offering above the paying of your tithe." —a true story by Jess Johnson

Date Used: _____

Regular Giving

I have heard many happy stories from people who have built into their family finances a sizable regular amount that they commit back to God. I have never yet heard anyone who made such a commitment complain about having done it!

Date Used: _____

A cartoon in a church paper showed a clergyman instructing the people in the use of the new computer terminals and credit card system that had been installed in the pew backs.

We get a chuckle out of that, but my next reaction is a feeling of disappointment. It cheats me! That method takes away a lot of the joy— putting back the offering, deciding against buying something or setting money aside with purpose. It's only a little-contemplated credit-card decision. It cheats God too!

Date Used: _____

Paul suggested to the Corinthians that they would bring their best offering for the poor Christians in Jerusalem if they laid aside some of it week by week.

His good thinking guides us today. Our vacation plans often materialize if we use that method. Many of us save money that way, much more than we would any other. And this method of giving for God's work will gather the most with relative ease.

God has instructed us through His apostle. We are blessed in the process.

Date Used: _____

The whole world has its hand out! It is one of my warmest joys to sit at the desk, gratefully note my paycheck, thank God for it, and, of my own will, thank Him for the privilege of taking a responsible part in His work as I prepare to give Sunday's offering back to Him.

Date Used: _____

The Lord responds to serious financial commitment in different ways. Sometimes He teaches us how to live poorer and enjoy it; sometimes He trains us in money use, so that less can actually become more; sometimes He gives us much more.

One young couple were new converts. He ran a grocery store. When they began to give, they committed seven dollars a week. Then, without his knowing it, his wife began to write the check for thirteen dollars, and for four weeks he began putting in an extra five dollars.

When they talked about it one day, and found that they had been giving eighteen dollars a week, they figured back to when they had started. It was the exact week when grocery receipts began to rise in a month when they ordinarily fall.

Date Used: _____

Sometimes you hear our national budget being talked about in terms of hundreds of billions of dollars. I can't imagine how much money that is. What you and I have seems so small. But without a bunch of little folks like us paying our taxes, such items wouldn't be.

Our church budget is a relatively small amount per year. That figure is small enough that I can understand it, but still large enough that it's hard to imagine how my bit is important. Still, the contributions of every member are vital to the whole church.

Date Used: _____

Paul talked to the Corinthians about their gift for the poor Christians in Jerusalem. "Let each one do just as he has proposed in his heart," he said.

That's the secret to a great ministry in missions, evangelism, benevolence, human service, building growth, and community outreach: each one of us sharing in the task with joy. We will grow as each one considers, plans, and gives.

Date Used: _____

Offering time leads us to make an examination of our stewardship. God cares also about how we make our money, how we spend it, and how we handle what we keep. The apostolic church stressed the importance of giving a regular proportion of all we take in.

But what expenditure do we make of time, of energy, of talent in work done for the Lord Jesus Christ? What ministry are we preparing for?

Date Used: _____

It's offering time! A good time!

Did you ever make a sand castle at the seashore? Maybe you went down close to the edge and took a big scoop out of the sand. Then the sea swept in, and when you looked down there was no hole.

That's just what happens when we give to take part in the church, an important expression of the kingdom of God. We give—then God fills up the hole again.

Date Used: _____

The Great
Giving Spirit

This week I visited a great university. The new buildings all around me were built with public funds gotten from not necessarily willing people. In some lands that's the way churches are maintained and clergymen paid. I praise the Lord that this is not our way. The taxation of reluctant people makes empty and lifeless churches. We're alive and strong because of happy and unpressured gifts that represent returned love.

Date Used: _____

Three persons watched the offering plate being passed.

One said, "There goes some of my hard earned money."

The second said, "It's my duty to give something to my church."

The third said, "What a privilege it is to support the building of God's kingdom."

What do you say when the plate comes to you?

Date Used: _____

Norman Vincent Peale offers some hints for building joy: First, *overcome something:* a fear, a jealousy, a grudge, or a temptation. The glow of happiness and satisfaction that follows will make you realize that real delight in life does not consist of giving in, but in getting over. Second, sing at least one song every day. This may not add to the enjoyment of your family or friends, but it will be a wonderful tonic for you.

Giving gets to be the real joy for us, too.

Date Used: _____

"The Lord loveth a cheerful giver, but He also accepteth from grouches."

God can guide the use of whatever resources we make available; but a gift cheerfully given is a great blessing to everyone touching the process—even the giver!

Date Used: _____

An eleven-year-old boy went to the neighbor's door with garden vegetables. "Would you like to buy some fresh squash?" he asked.

"I'm sorry, but we don't like squash very much," said the neighbor.

"I don't blame you," the boy answered. "I don't like it either."

That's not the way I approach the offering any more. I like giving. The King deserves it, His church deserves it, and we're a far richer family for the giving.

Try the squash. You'll like it!

Date Used: _____

The minister with a certain church used to visit newcomers in town who were of that faith. Not long after they began to get acquainted, he started to talk about their membership with the church. Then he asked how much the family's income was. When that information was reluctantly given, he proceeded to tell them what their pledge should be.

I think we are all glad that we don't use that method in our church. We give cheerfully, and God blesses both what is given and what is retained for our own use.

Date Used: _____

"Just this morning I read a fascinating account of an automobile accident in Britain. We are not alone in having such activities, of course. The auto has made 'blood brothers' of us all! However, this particular mishap was of special interest. It seems a sixty-nine-year-old woman lost control of her car near Bournemouth, the famous British seaside resort. The car crashed through a wire fence and hurtled off a cliff eighty feet high. During its descent it somersaulted three times, landed on its wheels, and then fell over on its side. The lady driver emerged, with some difficulty, and confronted some anxious spectators who had gathered around. Her first words were, 'Where's my purse?' " ("Thistle" in *Christian Standard*)

Money is important to us. The manner and spirit in which we handle it are important to God.

Date Used: _____

Here's a grand idea about how we can finance an addition to this building: One Sunday, while we are all inside here, someone can auction off all the cars in the parking lot!

That seems a little heavy-handed.

We realize that we are a people blessed in many, many ways, and that God is the source of all these blessings. To God's plan, the church is of tremendous importance.

Our gifts gladly display our determination that the church do all it can do, and we do not need the coercion of an auctioneer.

Date Used: _____

It's offering time! "Bye-bye, dear dollars!" some say, almost crying in the offering plates.

But not many. The people here happily take important financial partnership in a growing family that seeks to serve the cause of Jesus Christ.

We grow as we give more, and we also grow as more and more of us steadily give.

Date Used: _____

In *Leadership* magazine Fred Smith wrote about millionaire industrialist Maxey Jarman, who was also a giving Christian:

"He was afraid of accumulating personal wealth. He talked about money's deception and the evils it brought to those obsessed with it."

"He gave millions to Christian causes."

"He gave currently. He didn't save up for special occasions."

"Tithing was much too little for him to give."

"As close as we were, he never told me of a single gift he ever made, even though I know he offered as much as a million dollars to start a Bible college."

"Even when Maxey was at his lowest personal fortune, he gave a check for $13,000 to help Youth for Christ with a project."

"During the darkest days of his temporary financial crunch I asked him if he ever thought of the millions he had given away. 'Of course I have, but remember, I didn't lose a penny I gave away. I only lost what I kept.' "

(Fred Smith, "Something I Learned from Maxey Jarman," *Leadership*, Vol. 2, No. 1, Winter, 1981.)

Date Used: _____

Ronald J. Sider wrote a book called *Rich Christians in an Age of Hunger*. After reading the title we already know that we are not going to like very much of what he has to say.

About our giving he writes a paragraph well worth some thought:

"The Macedonians were extremely poor. Apparently they faced difficulties just when Paul asked for a generous offering (2 Corinthians 8:2). But still they gave beyond their means. No hint here of a mechanical ten percent for pauper and millionaire. Giving as much as you can is the Pauline pattern."

(Taken from *Rich Christians in an Age of Hunger* by Ronald J. Sider. Copyright 1977 by InterVarsity Christian Fellowship and used by permission of InterVarsity Press.)

Date Used: _____

An "Epistle from Thistle" in *Christian Standard* has an interesting tale about giving.

"It is said there once was a small boy who went to church with his mother, but was not accustomed to attending. Before the service his mother gave him some money he was to put in the offering plate when it was passed, and his mother indicated she would put some in too. As the service went on and on through hymns, announcements, prayer, and the Scripture reading, the boy became more and more restless. Finally he whispered to his mother, 'Mom, if we give him the money now, do you think he'll let us go?' ''

Sometimes we give painfully, sometimes with pretense, sometimes with no feeling. Sometimes we don't give at all!

Many here give with determination and with great delight. We give because we believe in the church. We want it to thrive and reach out. We want to give our best, and we rejoice in the personal blessing that comes from our giving.

Date Used: _____

One little first-grader that I heard about gives personality to the kind of spirit with which we should give to God. His church had a growth need, and the minister talked about it one Sunday, earnestly supporting the project. That afternoon our young friend, excited by the fact that "my church needs it," hurried upstairs to get the five-dollar bill his grandfather had given him for his birthday, and lovingly laid it aside for the offering next Sunday.

His parents report that there was never a moment's regret after he placed it enthusiastically in the offering plate. Can't you just see his eyes when he did? A worthy undertaking had been supported with the best he had.

Date Used: _____

Giving Thoughts
by Season

Easter and Springtime

Very little needs to be said to remind us of the significance of our giving today. The events of Easter jolt us to memory.

What a way to handle our sin; allowing the murder of His Son! What a wonderful promise, as Jesus shook off the bonds of death! Our personal gratitude, and the fact that we want others to know what God has brought about, prompt our giving today.

Date Used: _____

This week we have paid our taxes! We pass money to the government, then it is used for a variety of purposes, several of which benefit us. That's fair! We give, then the government gives back. (A slight amount is eaten up, but that's the way human institutions are!)

With God, He gives first, and gives, and gives, and gives—and in loving response we give back. That's the happier way, isn't it?

Date Used: _____

Sometimes at this season churches receive a "thirty pieces of silver" offering. Rather than betraying Jesus for that amount of silver, His disciples bring that amount as a way of honoring Him and sharing in the ministry of His church.

This kind of special offering has always struck me as a little negative, though, almost as if the gift is brought as an apology. Today we bring our gifts, not apologetically, but gladly, militantly. The giving does us a great deal of good. Since Christ has left the work of His body in human hands it is both a responsibility and a privilege for us to take part in the witness to Christ through His church.

Date Used: _____

It is that great time of year called "1040 Time." Uncle Sam calls for our help in financing the government. Some of us will file and give him more than we have already contributed, and some of us will wait to get a bit back.

One reminder that comes to us as we file is that the United States government believes that the church offers important things to society. That is why we are allowed to deduct our gifts to the church. Some of us have given more, and our tax bill will be less. Maybe we will think of that this year!

That, of course, is not our reason for giving. We will give even if the government stops seeing the importance of Christ's church. We see how important it is more clearly all the time as we grow.

Date Used: _____

I think that these are days when giving is easy! Yes, some of us have just made a quarterly tax payment, and vacations are coming up.

But God's blessings are evident. Haven't there been times recently when you walked outside in the pleasant evening air and thought to yourselves, "Boy, it's great to be alive!" All we have comes from God; and there is more (and better) still to come—His presence forever.

The church rejoices in these good days. We gratefully use God's good gifts and hear the call to service in His present kingdom, and we are anxious to announce His eternal kingdom. We gladly bring our part for sharing and spreading the life and witness, the growth, and the fellowship of Christ's church.

Date Used: _____

Vacations and Summer

Vacations are great, but the prices are something else. What could possibly be left for the offering? Two Sundays's worth! It's something of a strain on one's resources to come up with that amount, but the kingdom of Christ is certainly worth it.

Date Used: _____

After a week of vacation I felt like a first cousin to a cash register. It seemed that every hour I was walking up to look him in his rolling eyes and hear his jangling heart.

It's nice to come today and make an offering—to give willingly for the purposes of Christ, whose hand is on me for comfort, not reaching out to me for His own enrichment.

Date Used: _____

We are in the wedding season—a lot of excitement, a lot of money spent. Years ago, when I was married, it all cost about $1.50! Times change, and prices, and incomes. And it's all okay—just as long as we keep money and things in

their proper place; if we see that they are temporary tools used to promote higher purposes.

Date Used: _____

Sometimes our children have an interesting
perspective on money. One left a note in the
offering plate:

"Dear Minister,

I'm sorry I can't leave more money in the plate at
church on Sunday, but my father didn't give me a
raise in my allowance. Could you give a sermon
about a raise in allowance? It would help the
church get more money."

Sometimes they can teach us about using money.
Some kids will gladly take their whole allowance,
maybe more, to give to this week's VBS missionary.
Several will choose not to buy things for themselves in order to give the money to those mission
efforts, and won't feel sorry at all.

When we have experienced the joy of giving
(and we come to that point at different ages) what
we choose to bypass in order to share in the
kingdom's growth becomes of very little worth.
And the partnership holds greater value.

Date Used: _____

The typical picture of a Boy Scout shows him
helping a little old lady across the street, whether

she wants to go or not! Such a shallow look, of course, is a great disservice to a fine organization. Scouts will help ladies, men, brothers, and sisters by giving of themselves, and they will learn in the process that self-giving is the secret of fulfillment.

Even more, in the kingdom of Jesus Christ, we see that giving is the secret of fulfillment. In bringing gifts now, we follow the style of the King (used Boy Scout Sunday).

Date Used: _____

Election Time
and the Autumn

I hope that in the first week of November everyone here will vote for those people and issues that best represent Christian ideals and hopes for this community and country. I also hope we will be prepared to support our votes with solid citizenship.

On Sunday we cast a vote too. The simple fact of our attendance announces a vote for the church, and for discipleship that wants to learn more from Christ. People pay attention to that vote.

When we listen we vote, too. "Say, Mrs. Smith really listens when the preacher talks. Sometimes nods her head!" Someone else says, "Maybe I should listen better."

We cast a vote when we give our offering too. "I watch Mr. and Mrs. Jones, and every week they put an envelope in the offering," someone notices. "And one week I saw how much. Wow! That's something to think about."

Date Used: _____

Christmas and Winter

It's a new year. Soon we'll think about income tax—ouch!

It's January—can you imagine what the heating bill will be this month?

Social security taxes are up, and medical insurance.

Maybe you have a crippled car that must be fixed.

It seems that everyone has a piece of us. We have to pay! Isn't it great to give for God's kingdom, which we know is terribly important? Not grudging or of necessity, but deliberately and gladly, for that which is really right.

Date Used: _____

Have you been trampled yet this Christmas shopping season? You will be! People really seem anxious to spend their money.

Our financial secretary wasn't trampled last week, but at least he heard footsteps. Our special gifts reflected great love and joy. And more of you are learning the blessings of giving all the time. The gifts will be used to the glory of Christ.

Date Used: _____

With Christmas coming sometimes we feel we should warn, "Now, don't give God's part away to people on the Christmas list." Honestly, few of us have any intention of doing that. In fact, many happily reach new levels of sharing in the business of Christ's kingdom because of the season's sense of rejoicing and hope.

May your giving today mean something special to you.

Date Used: _____

Little more needs to be said at offering time this day than to direct our attention to one bulletin cover. That's why *our* giving has powerful significance. "Unto Us a Son is Given."

Date Used: _____

"A Gift"

A friend of mine named Paul received a new automobile from his brother as a Christmas present. On Christmas eve, when Paul came out of his office, a street urchin was walking around the shiny new car admiring it. "Is this your car, mister?" he asked.

Paul nodded. "My brother gave it to me for Christmas."

The boy was astounded. "You mean your brother gave it to you and it didn't cost you nothing? Boy, I wish . . ." he hesitated.

And Paul knew what he was going to wish. He was going to wish he had a brother like that. But what the lad said jarred Paul all the way down to his heels.

"I wish," the boy went on, "that I could *be* a brother like that."

Paul looked at the boy in astonishment, then impulsively he added, "Would you like to ride in my automobile?"

"Oh, yes, I'd like that."

After a short ride, the urchin turned and with his eyes aglow said, "Mister, would you mind driving in front of my house?"

Paul smiled a little. He thought he knew what the lad wanted. He wanted to show his neighbors that he could ride home in a big automobile. But Paul was wrong again.

"Will you stop where those two steps are?" the boy asked.

He ran up the steps. Then in a little while Paul heard him coming back but he was not coming fast. He was carrying his little polio-crippled brother. He sat him down on the bottom step, then sort of squeezed up against him and pointed to the car.

"There she is, Buddy, just like I told you upstairs. His brother give it to him for Christmas and it didn't cost him a cent. And some day I'm gonna give you one just like it. . . . Then you can see for yourself all the pretty things in the Christmas windows that I've been trying to tell you about."

Paul got out and lifted the little lad to the front seat of his car. The shining eyed older brother climbed in beside him and the three of them began a memorable holiday ride.

That Christmas eve Paul learned what Jesus meant when He said: "It is more blessed to give. . . ."

—author unknown

Date Used: _____